W9-AUS-494

nothing but
MIRACLES

nothing but

MIRACLES

From *Leaves of Grass*

by Walt Whitman
illustrated by Susan L. Roth

NATIONAL GEOGRAPHIC

Washington, D.C.

I know of nothing else
but miracles,

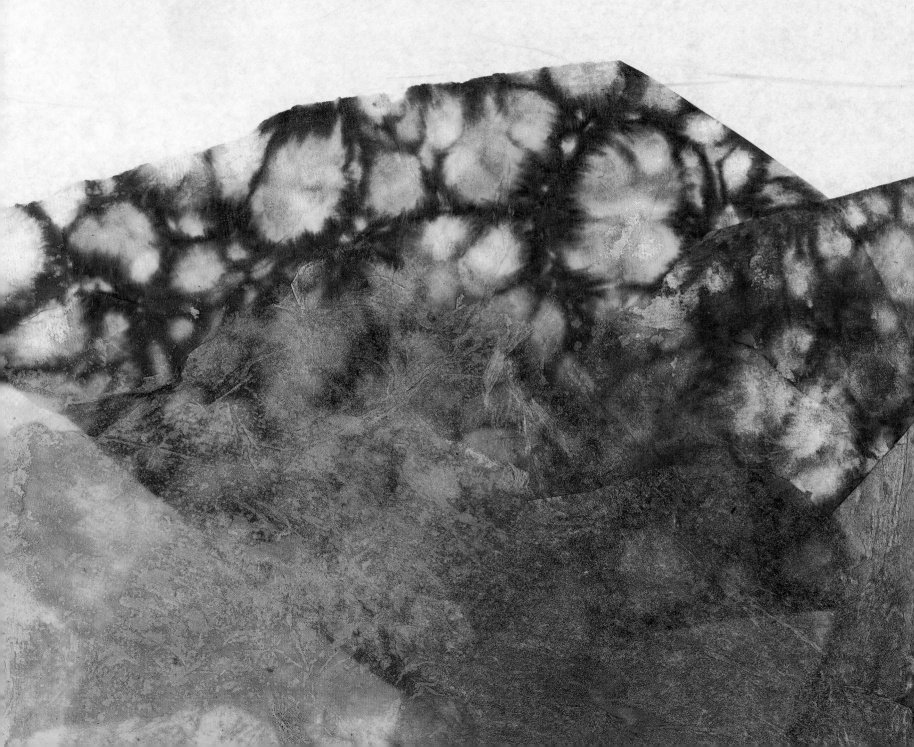

Whether I walk the streets of Manhattan,

Or dart my sight
over the roofs of houses
toward the sky,

Or wade with naked feet

along the beach
just in the edge of the water,

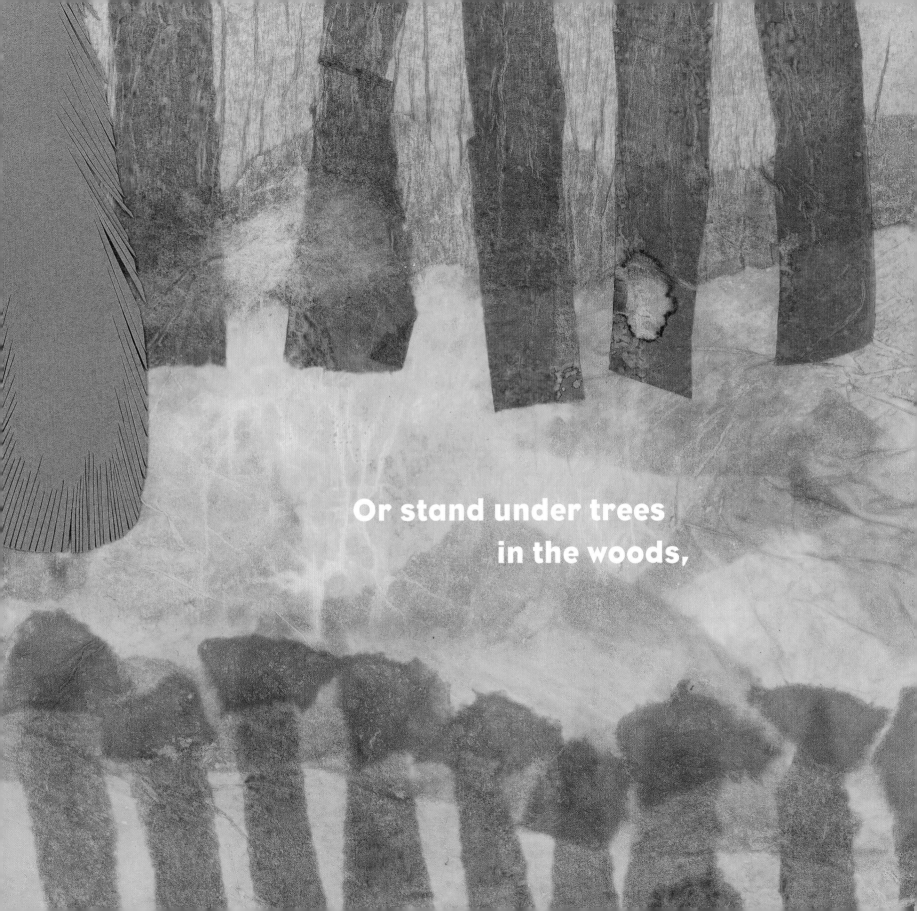

Or stand under trees
in the woods,

Or talk by day with any one I love,

or sleep in the bed at night
with any one I love,

Or sit at table at dinner with the rest,

Or look at strangers opposite me

riding in the car,

Or watch honey-bees busy around
the hive of a summer forenoon,
Or animals feeding in the fields,
Or birds,

or the wonderfulness of insects
in the air,

Or the wonderfulness
of the sundown,

or of stars shining so quiet
and bright,

Or the exquisite delicate thin curve
of the new moon in spring;

These with the rest,
one and all,
are to me miracles.

Illustrator's Note

The Collages

In this poem Walt Whitman draws together diverse wonders of life into a cohesive whole. For me, this is the essence of collage. It is what I try to do every time I choose a shard of paper, a treasure from the trove. As I collect my pieces, they might have even less to do with each other than sidewalks and beehives. But after the parts are joined together, I hope that with my head, hands, and heart, I have made them one.

For me, every piece of paper I save is a miracle. I love that the trunks of the trees on this page come from Portland, Oregon, that the leaves come from Amsterdam, the sky from Kyoto, the water from Baltimore. Papers are my paints and colored pencils.

It was nothing but a miracle for me to find Walt Whitman's collage of a poem and to be able to add my own collages to it.

The Poem

Whitman first published this poem in the 1856 edition of *Leaves of Grass* under the title "Poem of Perfect Miracles." He revised it several times in subsequent editions, changing its title to "Miracles." To illustrate *Nothing But Miracles* I have chosen a large segment of the poem, but here is the whole poem as it appeared in the 1886 edition of *Leaves of Grass* published by Walter Scott Publishers, London:

MIRACLES

WHY, who makes much of a miracle?
As to me, I know of nothing else but miracles,
Whether I walk the streets of Manhattan,
Or dart my sight over the roofs of houses toward the sky,
Or wade with naked feet along the beach just in the edge of the water,
Or stand under trees in the woods,
Or talk by day with any one I love, or sleep in the bed at night with any one I love,
Or sit at table at dinner with the rest,
Or look at strangers opposite me riding in the car,
Or watch honey-bees busy around the hive of a summer forenoon,
Or animals feeding in the fields,
Or birds, or the wonderfulness of insects in the air,
Or the wonderfulness of the sundown, or of stars shining so quiet and bright,
Or the exquisite delicate thin curve of the new moon in spring;
These with the rest, one and all, are to me miracles,
The whole referring, yet each distinct and in its place.

To me every hour of the light and dark is a miracle,
Every cubic inch of space is a miracle,
Every square yard of the surface of the earth is spread with the same,
Every foot of the interior swarms with the same.

To me the sea is a continual miracle,
The fishes that swim—the rocks—the motion of the waves—the ships with the men in them,
What stranger miracles are there?

Walt Whitman

Illustrations copyright © 2003 Susan L. Roth

Published by the National Geographic Society. All rights reserved.
Reproduction of the whole or any part of the contents without written
permission from the National Geographic Society is strictly prohibited.

Book design by Cindy Min
The text is set in Eagle-Book.

Library of Congress Cataloging-in-Publication Data
available upon request
ISBN 0-7922-6143-7

Printed in Belgium

One of the world's largest nonprofit scientific and educational organizations, the National Geographic Society was founded in 1888 "for the increase and diffusion of geographic knowledge." Fulfilling this mission, the Society educates and inspires millions every day through its magazines, books, television programs, videos, maps and atlases, research grants, the National Geographic Bee, teacher workshops, and innovative classroom materials. The Society is supported through membership dues, charitable gifts, and income from the sale of its educational products. This support is vital to National Geographic's mission to increase global understanding and pro-mote conservation of our planet through exploration, research, and education.

For more information, please call 1-800-NGS LINE (647-5463) or write to the
following address:

NATIONAL GEOGRAPHIC SOCIETY
1145 17th Street N.W.
Washington, D.C. 20036-4688 U.S.A.

Visit the Society's Web site: www.nationalgeographic.com